ALL ABOUT PASSOVER

JUDYTH GRONER
MADELINE WIKLER

ILLUSTRATED BY
KINNY KREISWIRTH

KAR-BEN COPIES, INC.
ROCKVILLE, MARYLAND

Acknowledgements

Sections of the "Story of Passover" are adapted from *My Very Own Haggadah* © 1974, 1983, 1999 by Judyth Groner and Madeline Wikler and *A Family Haggadah* © 1987 by Shoshana Silberman, both published by Kar-Ben Copies, Inc.

Library of Congress Cataloging-in-Publication Data

Groner, Judyth Saypol
 All About Passover / Judyth Groner; illustrated by Kinny Kreiswirth
    p.   cm.
Summary: Retells the story of Passover and the Israelites' flight from Egypt and explains the traditions of the Passover Seder today.
ISBN 1-58013-060-7
    1. Passover — Juvenile literature. 2. Seder— Juvenile Literature. [1. Passover. 2. Seder.] I. Kreiswirth, Kinny, ill.
BM695.P.3 G76 2000
296.4'37—dc21

99-057600

Published by KAR-BEN COPIES, INC.
6800 Tildenwood Lane · Rockville, MD 20852
1-800-4-KARBEN
Printed in the United States of America

CONTENTS

For lo the winter is past,
The rain is over and gone.
The flowers appear on the earth;
The time of singing is come.
— *Song of Songs*

Passover celebrates the coming of spring and the birth of the Jewish people as a nation. It was in the spring, over 3000 years ago, that the Jews were freed from slavery in Egypt.

The first Passover was observed just before the Jewish people fled from Pharaoh. Each family roasted a lamb and ate it with matzah and bitter herbs.

Today, Passover is celebrated for eight days,* starting on the evening of the 15th day of the Hebrew month Nisan (late March or April). The holiday begins with a festive meal called a seder when we read the story of the Exodus, the Jewish people's historic journey to freedom.

* Jews in Israel and some in the diaspora celebrate for seven days.

The Passover story begins when Joseph was sold into slavery by his brothers and came to be an official in the court of the Egyptian Pharaoh. Joseph's advice saved the land from a great famine. When Joseph's family came to Egypt in search of food, Pharaoh invited them to stay. They lived in peace for many years and became known as Israelites.

Years later, a new Pharaoh came to rule. He did not remember Joseph and all he had done for the Egyptians. He saw that the Israelite population was growing, and feared that in a war they might side with the enemy.

So Pharaoh made the Israelites slaves. He forced them to work hard building his cities and palaces. They knew neither peace nor rest, only misery and pain.

To limit the population, Pharaoh decreed that every baby boy born to an Israelite woman be drowned in the river.

One couple, Amram and Yocheved, hid their baby in a basket on the riverbank. When Pharaoh's daughter, the princess, came down to the river to bathe, she found the baby and decided to take him home to the palace.

Miriam, the baby's sister, saw the princess rescue her brother and asked if she needed a baby nurse. The princess said yes. Miriam told her mother, and so it happened that Yocheved was able to care for her son and teach him about his people.

The princess named the baby Moses. In Hebrew his name means "brought out of the water."

Moses could have lived at the Pharaoh's palace forever, but he could not bear to watch the suffering of the Jewish slaves. He left Egypt and became a shepherd in a faraway land.

One day when Moses was taking care of his sheep, he saw a burning bush and heard God's voice coming from the bush. God told Moses to go back to Egypt to free the Israelites and take them away from cruel Pharaoh.

Moses returned to Egypt. He went to see Pharaoh and told him, "Let my people go." But Pharaoh refused to listen to him.

God was angry with Pharaoh and punished him ten times. These punishments were called plagues. Each punishment frightened Pharaoh, and each time he promised to free the slaves. But he did not keep his word. Finally, after the last plague, the death of the first-born sons of the Egyptians, Pharaoh agreed to let the Israelites go.

The people got ready quickly. They didn't have time to bake bread for their journey. Instead, they put raw dough on their backs. The sun baked it into hard crackers called matzah. The Jewish people followed Moses to the banks of the sea.

Soon after Pharaoh let the slaves leave, he changed his mind and ordered his army to bring them back. Pharaoh's soldiers caught up with the Israelites by the banks of the sea.

God told Moses to hold up his walking stick. When he did, a strong wind parted the sea, and the people were able to walk across on dry land. The Egyptians came after them into the sea. Moses again lifted his stick, and the waters rushed back, covering the Egyptians and their horses and chariots.

When the people were safely out of Egypt, Moses and his sister Miriam led them in songs of thanks to God.

PASSOVER TODAY

The name *Passover* (*Pesach* in Hebrew) is taken from the story of the Exodus from Egypt. When Pharaoh refused Moses' request to free the Jewish people, God brought plagues on the Egyptians. During the tenth plague, God struck down the first-born sons of the Egyptians, but he *passed over* the homes of the Jews. That night Pharaoh finally agreed to let the Jewish people go free. Thus, Passover is also called the *time of our freedom.*

Another name for Passover is the *holiday of matzah.* The Torah commands us to eat matzah, to recall how our ancestors had to leave Egypt in such a hurry that the dough for their bread did not have time to rise.

CHAMETZ

The Torah commands us to remove all *chametz* from our homes during Passover as a reminder that the Jewish slaves had no time to let their dough rise in their hurry to leave Egypt.

Chametz, that which we are forbidden to eat on Passover, is a mixture of flour and water that has been allowed to ferment, or to rise. It also includes foods made from such a mixture, such as bread, rolls, cookies, and pasta.

Before Passover, many Jewish families engage in spring cleaning. They scour the house from top to bottom to get rid of all chametz. They pack up or give away unopened chametz, and fill the cupboards with special Passover foods. Some families also take out special dishes, pots and pans used only on Passover.

Not only can't we eat chametz during Passover, we should not own any. Thus traditional Jews "sell" their chametz to non-Jews for the week of the holiday. They use a contract created by the rabbis for this purpose.

The rabbis say that chametz — dough that has been allowed to puff up — is a reminder of how we can get puffed up and self-important. Getting rid of chametz before Passover reminds us to think about getting rid of our false pride.

SEARCHING FOR CHAMETZ

On the evening before the first seder we make a final check to be sure that no chametz has been overlooked. Then we conduct a *bedikah*, a search for chametz. One member of the family hides small pieces of bread throughout the house. Other family members, carrying a candle (or flashlight) to show the way, a feather to use as a brush, and a wooden spoon to catch the bread, search the house and collect the pieces.

The following blessing is said before the search:

בָּרוּךְ אַתָּה יְיָ אֱלֹהֵינוּ מֶלֶךְ הָעוֹלָם,
אֲשֶׁר קִדְּשָׁנוּ בְּמִצְוֹתָיו וְצִוָּנוּ עַל בִּעוּר חָמֵץ.

Baruch Atah Adonai Eloheinu Melech ha'olam, asher kidshanu b'mitzvotav v'tzivanu al bei'ur chametz.

Blessed are You, Adonai, for the mitzvah of searching for chametz.

After the search we declare:

Any chametz which I have not seen or removed shall be considered as the dust of the earth.

The next morning the bread we have collected is burned.

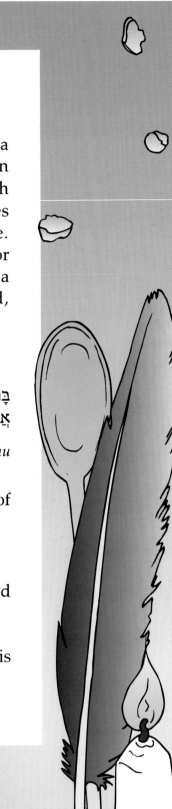

MATZAH

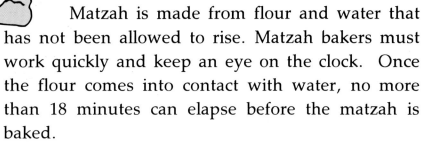

Matzah is made from flour and water that has not been allowed to rise. Matzah bakers must work quickly and keep an eye on the clock. Once the flour comes into contact with water, no more than 18 minutes can elapse before the matzah is baked.

Flour and water are placed in a tub and mixed to form a dough. The dough is kneaded for about a minute and rolled out thin and flat. Then a special machine perforates the matzah with tiny holes to prevent it from rising in the oven. Finally, the matzah is rushed to a hot oven for baking.

Some families use only hand-baked matzah made from flour that has been watched from the time the wheat is harvested. This matzah is called *shmurah* matzah (guarded matzah).

Once matzah is baked, it can be ground into meal. Matzah meal is used to make cookies and cakes that can be eaten during Passover.

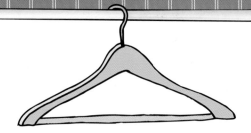

TZEDAKAH AT PASSOVER

At the beginning of the seder, we invite all who are hungry to come and join us. Though we really don't expect strangers to walk through the door, this reading reminds us of our need to make sure that all Jews are able to celebrate Passover.

We, who are free from want, who have food to eat, clothes to wear, and a place to live, must make an effort to care for those in need.

An important mitzvah is *ma'ot chittim* (wheat money). Rabbis collect funds to purchase matzah, wine, and food for needy families so they can have a seder.

In many places, travelers and newcomers are invited to family or communal seders. Seders are held for people living in hospitals and nursing homes, on college campuses and army bases.

Synagogues sponsor food collections, and encourage families to donate unopened boxes of chametz — cookies, cereal, and pasta — to local food pantries.

Passover spring cleaning is a good time to gather up clothes and toys that family members have outgrown and to donate these items to homeless shelters.

THE SEDER

We begin our celebration of Passover as it was observed in the time of Moses...with a meal called a seder.

A seder is not just a dinner party. Before our meal, we read from a special book, the Haggadah. Through stories, songs, and blessings the Haggadah tells the story of the Exodus.

The rabbis say that when we tell the story, we should begin with sadness and end with joy. We begin with the story of our people as slaves in Egypt and end with their crossing the sea to freedom.

The purpose of the seder is to make each participant feel as though he or she was among those Jewish slaves who left Egypt. As we tell the story, eat the special foods, and drink the four cups of wine, we feel part of Jewish history.

Anyone can lead a seder. In some families, the oldest guest is the leader; in others, the participants take turns reading from the Haggadah and leading the songs and prayers.

No two seders are alike. Some last for an hour, others for three. Each family creates its own traditions.

THE HAGGADAH

In ancient times, the seder was mainly a feast. Each year, to commemorate the Exodus, families roasted a lamb and ate it with matzah and maror. But the rabbis said that whoever elaborates on the story of the Israelites journey to freedom is to be commended. So over the years, prayers, poems, and stories were added.

Haggadah means "to tell." It comes from the passage in the Torah that commands us to "tell" our children about the Exodus. The text includes passages from the Bible, as well as songs, stories, blessings, and commentary.

Over 3,000 versions of the Haggadah have been published. New editions are produced each year. Many include beautiful illustrations. The book has been translated into over 20 languages spoken in countries where Jews have lived through the ages. There are versions in braille and large type for those with vision problems. Special Haggadahs have been written for children.

THE SEDER TABLE

The seder table is different from a regular supper table. There are three pieces of matzah covered with a cloth, a bowl of salt water for dipping foods, an extra cup of wine for Elijah, and a seder plate with special foods.

THE SEDER PLATE

BEITZAH
Roasted Egg

A reminder of spring and new life

KARPAS
Green Vegetable

A symbol of spring, the time of the Exodus

MAROR
Bitter Herb

Recalls the bitter life of the Jewish slaves

ZEROA
Roasted Bone

Recalls the lamb which the Israelites roasted and ate at the first Passover

CHAROSET
Chopped Apples and Nuts

Recalls the mortar used by slaves to build Pharaoh's cities

THE ORDER OF THE SEDER

Seder means "order."
We follow a certain order in telling the story.

1. KADDESH
Say Kiddush and drink the first cup of wine.

2. UR'CHATZ
Wash the hands.

3. KARPAS
Say the blessing and eat a vegetable dipped in salt water.

4. YACHATZ
Break the middle matzah and hide the larger half, the afikomen.

5. MAGGID
Tell the story of Passover, ask the Four Questions, drink the second cup of wine.

6. RACHTZAH
Wash the hands and recite a blesssing.

7. MOTZI MATZAH
Say the blessings and eat the matzah.

8. MAROR
Say the blessing
and eat the maror.

9. KORECH
Eat a sandwich of matzah
and bitter herbs.

10. SHULCHAN ORECH
Eat the festive meal.

11. TZAFUN
Find the hidden afikomen
and share it for dessert.

12. BARECH
Say the blessing after the meal,
drink the third cup of wine, and
welcome the prophet Elijah.

13. HALLEL
Sing songs of praise, ending with
the fourth cup of wine.

14. NIRTZAH
Complete the seder with song.

YOU SHALL TELL YOUR CHILDREN

Four times the Torah commands parents to teach the story of the Exodus to their children. From the beginning, the seder has highlighted the participation of children, and parts of the seder are designed especially for them.

AFIKOMEN

At the beginning of the seder the middle matzah is broken, and half is set aside for dessert. It is called the *afikomen*. To keep children awake until the end of the seder, matzah-hiding games are played. At some seders, the leader hides the afikomen and the children search for it. At others, the children steal the afikomen and the leader must offer a reward to get it back.

THE FOUR QUESTIONS

We introduce the Passover story
with Four Questions, traditionally
asked by the youngest child in the family.
Children are encouraged to ask more questions
about the unusual things we do as the seder
continues.

OPENING THE DOOR
FOR ELIJAH

There is an extra cup of wine on the seder
table. It is the Cup of Elijah. There is a
story that Elijah, a great teacher who
lived many years ago, visits each
seder to wish everyone a year of
peace. A child is asked to open
the door and invite Elijah to
come in. The children watch
his cup to see if any of the
wine disappears.

THE FOUR QUESTIONS

The Four Questions introduce the *maggid*, the storytelling part of the seder. They are designed as sample questions children may ask to learn about the story of Passover.

מַה נִּשְׁתַּנָּה הַלַּיְלָה הַזֶּה מִכָּל־הַלֵּילוֹת!

Ma nishtanah halailah hazeh mikol haleilot!

How different this night is from all other nights!

1. *On all other nights we eat all kinds of bread and crackers. Why do we eat only matzah on Pesach?*

The Answer: Matzah reminds us that when the Israelites left Egypt, they had no time to let their dough rise to bake bread for their journey. Instead, they put raw dough on their backs and the sun baked it into hard crackers called matzah.

2. *On all other nights we eat all kinds of vegetables and herbs. Why do we eat bitter herbs, maror, at our seder?*

The Answer: Maror reminds us of the bitter and cruel way Pharaoh treated the Israelites by forcing them to be slaves in Egypt.

3. *On all other nights we don't usually dip foods. Tonight we dip parsley in salt water and bitter herbs in charoset Why do we dip twice at our seder?*

The Answer: We dip bitter herbs into charoset (chopped apples and nuts) to remind us how hard the Jewish slaves worked in Egypt. Charoset looks like the clay used to make bricks to build Pharaoh's palaces. We also dip parsley into salt water. Parsley reminds us that it is spring and new life will grow. Salt water reminds us of the tears of the Jewish slaves.

4. *On all other nights we eat sitting up. Why do we lean on a pillow tonight?*

The Answer: We lean on a pillow to be comfortable and to remind us that once we were slaves, but now we are free.

THE REST OF PASSOVER

The Seder begins a week of celebration. Traditional Jews observe Passover for eight days. Seders are held on the first two nights. The first two and last two days are full holidays when no work is performed.

The in-between days, called *chol hamo'ed*, are half holidays. Synagogue services include a special Torah reading and Hallel songs of praise. A special kiddush over wine is recited on the Shabbat during Passover.

COUNTING THE OMER

Passover celebrates an important time in history, but it is also a celebration of nature.

In ancient Israel, Passover marked the beginning of the barley harvest. On the second day of the holiday, everyone brought an *omer*, a sheaf of barley, to the Holy Temple in Jerusalem. From that day, 49 days were counted until the beginning of the holiday of Shavuot, the holiday that commemorates the giving of the Torah on Mt. Sinai.

The fact that Jewish tradition links the two holidays of Passover and Shavuot shows that our freedom from slavery was not complete until we received the Torah, the rules which give our lives order and meaning.

The Omer is counted in the evening, beginning with the second seder.

Matzah Meal Latkes

½ c. matzah meal
¾ c. water
1 tsp. salt
3 eggs
oil for frying
1 diced apple (optional)
cinnamon-sugar mixture

Beat eggs well. Add matzah meal, water, salt, and apples. Drop by spoonfuls into hot oil and fry on both sides. Serve with cinnamon-sugar or jelly.

Matzah Toppers

Cinnamon-Orange Butter

½ c. softened butter
1 tsp. grated orange peel
1 Tbsp. orange juice concentrate
½ tsp. cinnamon
2 Tbsp. brown sugar

Strawberry Butter

½ c. softened butter
½ c. strawberries
1 Tbsp. sugar

Honey Butter

¼ c. softened butter or margarine
4 Tbsp. honey

Combine all ingredients and blend until smooth.

Veggie Fritters

½ c. each chopped mushrooms, celery, onion, red and green pepper, carrots
1 pkg. frozen spinach, cooked and drained
2 Tbsp. margarine
3 beaten eggs
¾ c. matzah meal
salt and pepper to taste
oil for frying

Saute vegetables in margarine until soft. Combine with rest of ingredients. Refrigerate for 10-20 minutes. Drop by spoonfuls into hot oil and fry on both sides.

Matzah Brei

4 matzah
4 beaten eggs
½ c. milk or water
oil for frying

Rinse matzah under cold running water. Press dry between sheets of paper towel. Mix eggs and milk and break matzah into bowl. Let sit 5-10 minutes. Fry in hot oil, stirring until set.

Passover Subs

1 c. water
¼ tsp. salt
½ c. oil
1 c. matzah meal
4 eggs

Boil water, oil, and salt. Remove from heat and stir in matzah meal. Add eggs, beating well after each. Shape into sub rolls and bake at 400º for 20-30 minutes until brown. Cool.

Cut rolls and spread with mayo, ketchup or other condiments. Layer lettuce, tomato, and your favorite meats, veggies, or cheese.

Apple Cake

4 small apples, peeled and sliced, tossed with 1 tsp. cinnamon and
½ c. sugar
3 eggs
1/3 c. oil
¼ c. sugar
¼ c. orange juice
1 c. matzah cake meal
½ tsp. salt

Beat eggs with orange juice and oil. Add sugar and stir in cake meal. Oil a 9-inch square pan. Spread half the batter in pan. Cover with half the apples. Spread rest of batter and top with rest of apples. Bake in 350º oven 50-60 minutes or until brown. Cut while warm.

Matzah Pizza

1 matzah
¼ c. tomato sauce
cheese slices
Slices of mushroom, green pepper, onion

Spread tomato sauce on matzah. Top with sliced cheese. Cover with veggies. Place on foil or foil-covered baking sheet and bake at 375º for 5 minutes or until cheese is melted.

Charoses Sundae

3 scoops ice cream
2 Tbsp. chopped walnuts
1/2 medium apple, cored and chopped
1/2 tsp. cinnamon
2 Tbsp. honey
2 Tbsp. red wine (optional)

Scoop the ice cream into dessert bowls. Combine rest of ingredients and sprinkle on top.

Carrot Apple Pudding

8 carrots, peeled and grated
3 apples, peeled and chopped
1 c. raisins
1/2 c. chopped nuts
4 eggs
1 c. matzah cake meal
2/3 c. oil
1 c. brown sugar
1 tsp. each cinnamon, salt
1/4 c. orange juice

Mix all ingredients. Pour into two greased loaf pans. Cover with foil. Bake at 325º for one hour. Reduce heat to 150º and bake for eight hours or overnight.

Chocolate Chip Cookies

1 ½ c. brown sugar
½ c. white sugar
1 tsp. Passover vanilla
1 c. margarine
2 eggs
¼ tsp. salt
½ c. matzah meal
½ c. matzah cake meal
1 c. potato starch
2 c. chocolate chips
parchment paper for baking

Cream sugars together with margarine and vanilla. Mix in eggs. Stir in dry ingredients and chocolate chips. Chill dough for at least 2 hours. Line cookie sheets with parchment paper. Form dough into tiny balls about the size of a marble and place on cookie sheet, leaving room for cookies to spread. Bake in preheated oven 10-12 minutes. Let cool 15-20 minutes before removing with spatula.

Published by KAR-BEN COPIES, INC.

ISBN 1-58013-060-7

EAN

9 781580 130608

50595